DEMOS

KU-603-416

Demos is an independent think-tank committed
to radical thinking on the long-term problems
facing the UK and other advanced industrial societies.

It aims to develop the ideas – both theoretical and
practical – that will help to shape the politics of the
21st century, and to improve the breadth and
quality of political debate.

Demos publishes books and a quarterly journal
and undertakes substantial empirical and policy-
oriented research projects. Demos is a registered charity.

In all its work Demos brings together people from
a wide range of backgrounds in business, academia,
government, the voluntary sector and the media to
share and cross-fertilise ideas and experiences.

For further information and
subscription details please write to:
Demos
9 Bridewell Place
London EC4V 6AP
Telephone: 0171 353 4479
Facsimile: 0171 353 4481
email: ...@demos.demon.co.uk

The Battle over Britain

Philip Dodd

DEM☉S

First published in 1995 by
Demos
9 Bridewell Place
London EC4V 6AP
Telephone: 0171 353 4479
Facsimile: 0171 353 4481
© Demos 1995

Paper No. 13
ISBN 1 898309 26 4
Printed in Great Britain by
EG Bond
Designed by Esterson Lackersteen

Contents

Introduction

Once upon a time, and not very long ago, nationalism
was something that took place elsewhere, or so it was
said. The British were properly patriotic of course,
but nationalistic, never. Well, give or take the odd
outburst of 'Celtic enthusiasm'. All that has changed
and a new Battle over Britain has been joined since
Mrs Thatcher staked her standard on the ground of
Britishness, claimed that 'we have ceased to be a nation
in retreat' and discovered and mobilised a British People
and a sense of Britishness that unnerved some and
uplifted others.

The 80s were the best of times and the worst of times;
a period when the institutions and industries that bore
the name of the British people – all the way from British
Gas to the Arts Council of Great Britain – were put in the
dock; a period when privatisation went hand in hand
with an increasingly centralised British state; a period
when a Prime Minister seemed to mean it when she said
she wanted to put the Great back into Britain, even if this
meant war; and when so much that had passed since the
postwar settlement as British commonsense was shown
to be not at all common and to have very little sense.

It may be that we can now see that the Thatcherite

project failed, broken by the contradiction between two mutually exclusive commitments – a political one to national sovereignty and an economic one to global imperatives. But even if it has failed, it has placed the question of Britishness at the centre of the agenda, put to flight the too often unexamined corporate Britishness that had previously reigned, and has imagined a new Britain, more demotic, populist and potentially more democratic, if more unnerving.

Certainly, even if Mrs Thatcher is no longer in power, the signs of the continuing Battle over Britain and its national identity are everywhere, not least in the political parties. They are most visible in the Tory Party which seems intent on tearing itself apart over what kind of Britain it wants – and whether European Union threatens national sovereignty and thus the historical identity of the British. Ghosts of Britishness past haunt the Party: in one corner there's Mr Major, trying to hang on to his Baldwinite love of country and cricket and Constitution, and at the same time negotiate his way into the heart of Europe; while in the other, Michael Portillo defends a kind of Britishness that we have learnt to call Thatcherite, but which actually has deep historical roots within a culture that has long defined itself in terms of its superiority to its 'untrustworthy neighbours'.

The battle over Britishness is beginning to look equally troublesome within the Labour Party, particularly as the constitutional implications of its stance on Europe sink in, and its commitment to radical decentralisation, which will see a parliament for Scotland and an assembly for Wales, but also possibly more self-government for the English regions. After all, ghosts of Britishness past haunt the Labour Party just as much as the Tory – perhaps above all the ghosts of 1945, of nationalisation and of a vision of a United Radical People, stretching back from the Suffragettes through the Chartists to the Levellers. All these ghosts are likely to be glimpsed over the next couple of years if, as seems evident, both of the major political parties make British national identity the declared battleground of the next election. Mr Blair claims that devolution both answers to the new needs of the British and will best protect the Union, while Mr Major is on record as saying that the proposals for devolution undermine the Constitution and preface the break-up of the United Kingdom. Since this was one of the songs he sang most effectively and passionately during the last election campaign, he is likely to give voice to it even more fulsomely at the next.

But the Battle over Britain and Britishness has also been staged in less obviously political places than Parliament. Indeed it may be the abiding limitation of politicians to believe that a new layer of government, its absence or even new Constitutional arrangements is a *sufficient* response to the crisis over national identity. It isn't. National identity matters precisely because it stretches far beyond the ceremonies of state into the very idioms of the language, and even into the way we hold our bodies. If the issue of the national identities of those who live in these islands is to be resolved, it will have to be done across all aspects of our lives, and not merely in the formal political part.

Certainly national identity has haunted civil society as much as political institutions. It's been there in the schools and in the continuing arguments over the national curriculum. Driving the debates around the curriculum for History or English are arguments such as: Who are the British? Which history should be taught? How national should it be? What are the crucial dates and events? Should literature in the English language be the subject of study or literature produced within Britain? It's been equally tangible in rows over the shape of new buildings. When Prince Charles weighed in saying that developers were threatening to do to St Paul's what the Luftwaffe could never do, then we could be in no doubt that memories of national defence were being mobilised.

The battle is also going on in the streets, in a more literal fashion. It's there in the escalating number of racial attacks on the black British, fuelled by a conviction that those who complicate the simple equation British=white deserve all the hatred they get; it's equally there, as a subtext, in the increasing anxiety over the 'swamping' of county cricket clubs by foreign players with the consequent damage to the English national side. It's also there in the agonised response to the 'decline of standards' and the sleaze that sticks to British politicians, the royal family and sports personalities alike. It's been there in the debates over the BBC, that voice of Britain, and over its continuing right to bring us together to share national events such as Wimbledon; it's even there in the claims that the British have lost their emotional moorings and a once patient and orderly people have become a disorderly rabble.

But Britishness is not simply the issue of the hour. No moratorium on thinking about who the British are will make everything well. The reasons for the present self-consciousness are many and they are simply not going to go away. They would probably include the fact that Britain no longer enjoys status as a world power, whatever explanations are proffered to make sense of its decline; that attempts to halt its economic decline never quite seem to work; that postwar immigration has thrown into relief an imperial history that has been repressed, and shown the British to be not quite as tolerant as they have imagined themselves to be; that demands for more autonomy from Scotland and Wales, not to mention the war in Northern Ireland, have thrown into question the claim that a single Britishness is subscribed to in all these countries; that closer union with Europe threatens to annul Britain's specialness; that with the rest of Europe convulsed by national and ethnic questions, Britain could not fail to be involved; and that the globalisation of the economy has made nations – including the British nation – wonder about their long-term survival.

One response to the turmoil is to view Britain and Britishness as anachronistic embarrassments and to jettison them – much as companies such as BA and BT have done. Yet while this may be seductive, we had better make sure that we know what we are doing. To say goodbye to Britishness and Britain will be to say goodbye to part of ourselves; it won't be easy even if we persuade ourselves it is desirable.

Goodbye to all that

To recognise that Britain and its identity are now in turmoil is not to say that it has ever been simply a given. But the issue of national identities within these islands does undoubtedly arise most intensely, as now, at moments of change – whether it is the early sixteenth century and the English King Henry VIII's break with Rome, the 1640s and the English civil war, the late seventeenth and early eighteenth century with King Billy, constitutional monarchy and the Union between Scotland and England, or the early 1800s, when patriotism became the cement to hold together a people in the face of the revolution in France. Or take a moment nearer our own: the years around the turn of this century. This, too, was a period of massive social change for Britain, with the need to accommodate new political institutions such as the Labour Party into the national life; military conflict from Ireland to South Africa; a self-conscious imperial Britain that had to make sense of its identity both to itself and the subjected peoples; the emergence of mass communications linking the nation together in new ways; and economic battles with European countries. And together with such change went, as now, a torrent of institutional and other reflections on national identity, from the setting up of the National Portrait Gallery to the reinvention of Queen Victoria as Empress of India in 1877, from the settlement of the Welsh Colleges that make up the University of Wales to the founding of the National Trust, from changes to the political franchise to the invention of English Literature as a subject at Oxford University. As Britain modernised, it had to reinvent itself. As now.

The issue is of course that the British identity stabilised in the late nineteenth century is hardly suitable for the British in the twenty- first century. But nor is another, and more attractive identity; the one forged during World War II and referred to in the Queen's most recent Christmas speech to the Commonwealth. But it is no disrespect to that time to say that the memory of such a United People (and let us for the moment not challenge the claim) is simply not likely to be effective to the generation coming to adulthood in 2000, who were born, like my own child in 1981 and for whom the Falklands, let alone the Second World War, is not even a memory. But at least as important is the question of whether a single unifying identity – the British People – is ever possible outside of the conditions of war, when the enemy is opposed with a call to arms. And even if it were possible, would it be desirable? After all, when The British People are now invited by the neo-fascists to rise up against other non-white British citizens, people born and legally settled here, how much should we want to engender a single unified Britishness that is so confident about who counts as 'us' and who as 'them'? To put it simply, its costs may be too high.

So this is the crisis: the need to imagine a usable national identity for the next century. But there is also a further crisis: the failure of the leading political and cultural elites to contribute to such an imagining. They are part of the problem. Above all, it is they who are dispirited, who have gathered up the sense of loss and decline – and no wonder, since it is their own loss and decline and the passing away of their sense of Britishness that they are in part mourning. The nearest analogue that comes to the mind is the late 1920s, when an exhausted generation of British men looked back and saw only loss and failure. It was the moment of the First World War literary memoirs, of Sassoon's *Memoirs of an Infantry Officer*, of Blunden's *Undertones of War*, of Robert Graves' *Goodbye to All That*; it was the aftermath of the General Strike; the moment when George Dangerfield was beginning to write *The Strange Death of Liberal England*; it was the time when 'Edwardian England' began to be invented, against all the available evidence, as a peaceful, quiet pastoral world (much as the 50s is imagined now).

Unlike men in the late 1920s, women who had finally gained the vote saw the moment, not in terms of such loss but of possibility, with a masculine sense of Britishness apparently giving way to a more feminine and domestic sense. Of course all analogues are partial but it is difficult not to feel that a generational and gender specific (and perhaps even English) sense of loss is now, as then, being offered as the whole story. When David Starkey, of the London School of Economics and of Radio 4's 'Moral Maze', said recently in *The Guardian*, 'England is dead', how much was he simply mourning himself and the passing of his world?

It is certainly true that an appetite for the future is hardly what has distinguished our political culture in the postwar period. In that perception Mrs Thatcher was right. Working according to custom and precedent as much as does English law, the measure of the success of the political future has too often been how much like the past it could look. After all, before the deluge of Thatcher, the Tories were prone to speak of the nation's thousand years of uninterrupted history and of themselves as its guardian. Labour was often not much better: until the success of Thatcher shook its complacency, it was wedded to the sacredness of its own (often undemocratic) traditions with a passion that would have gladdened the heart of anyone featured in Debrett's. The tenacity with which the leading cultural institutions – from the BBC through the older Universities to the Arts Council – have resisted *any* change, and their inability to imagine a future different from the past, has been a sign that they are in the short term unlikely to nurture the new. Such a political and cultural Britain has had increasingly to live on its memories – and the more it has been put in the dock through the Thatcher years the more tenaciously it has held to them. Some of these memories hark back to a time when there was a quiet, decent, yeoman people whose heroes were footballers such as Bobby Moore, serving his club and country with exemplary distinction; yet others hymn a radical people who have defended their own liberties and extended the world's; yet another laments the death of the service ethic in British public life, once the envy of the world. Some of the memories are less directly of people than places, yet these are places redolent of a particular nation. There are the villages of Wiltshire, before the lager louts and rural violence; the miners' terraced homes that ran along the South Wales valleys; small redbrick Universities that were real communities; the balcony of Buckingham Palace, with the Queen and her family greeting the people.

Over the last twenty years or so it has become de rigeur on the part of some of us to show how partial, unstable or downright invented so many of these memories are. For instance, to take the yeoman England that Bobby Moore represented. It's not merely that during his reign there were the bribery football scandals that throw what is happening now into the shade. It's also that in remembering Moore we are in danger of ignoring his near-contemporary and a rather different role model: the Welsh player John Charles, who was born and bred in Wales, moved to Leeds United and then to the Italian side Juventus where he became an Italian national hero, at the same time as remaining the backbone of the Welsh national side. But Charles is an awkward hero, not least because he is hard to fit into the story the British are told: that they are a settled and insular people.

It would be equally easy to show how partial are many of the other memories by which the British have warmed themselves in the encroaching cold. It has been the road to many a reputation to show that the monarchical spectacle for which the British are famed was invented as recently as the last quarter of the nineteenth century: that the short kilt, that icon of Scottishness, was the invention of an Englishman; and that the much vaunted claim that Britain is the fount of democracy is countered by the historical record showing that Britain was one of the least democratic countries up until the First World War. Each claim that some traditional virtue is passing away has been met by the pantomimic counter-claim, 'Oh no, it's not traditional'. When someone says that the working class are no longer the decent group they were twenty years ago, the riposte comes that the decent, quiet working class always retreat down the corridors of history as one chases them. So, if for Richard Hoggart in *The Uses of Literacy* in the late 50s, the decent working class were active in the 30s, for George Orwell writing in the 30s they were to be located in their domestic tranquillity before the First World War. Unfortunately during the Edwardian period they were thin on the ground according to the American observer Jack London: 'A new race has sprung up, a street people. The traditional silent and reserved Englishman has passed away. The pavement folk are noisy, voluble, high-strung and excitable'. And before anyone says that at least the British have always queued in an orderly fashion, unlike our European counterparts, it should be said that in the mid-nineteenth century, the English were called a hysterical people, by nature incapable of queuing.

Valuable and necessary as such historical enquiry has been, it has tended to be more powerful in unravelling the existing stories than in helping to shape new ones. And it is important to say that these deconstructions have come from what have been traditionally both left and right. Take the Second World War as an example. While the left was urgently showing that the United Britons of the war were a myth, that class antagonisms were alive and kicking, the right in a figure such as Correlli Barnett in *The Audit of War* was disclosing that the War was a massive disaster for Britain and that the political class in control, gentlemanly amateurs to a man, took no notice of economic imperatives and therefore bequeathed to the postwar generations the economic and cultural crises that followed.

Too often the writers have tended to assume that if the myths, stories and memories by which the British have lived were shown to be of recent origin rather than ancient, they would simply be abandoned – for all the world as if they were no more important than the belief that it may rain tomorrow. To stay with the meteorological metaphor, it would be more accurate to say they are more of the order of the air we breathe. To assume people would simply abandon the things by which they think and feel about their lives was naive at best, since people will only voluntarily leave their home if they have somewhere else to go. At worst, it did not recognise that even if those beliefs were historically unfounded or partial, there would need to be a space in which their passing could be recognised and even mourned. Nor that this is as important as the imperative to construct new stories that could answer to people's present needs and histories better than the old. I say this as someone brought up in a mining family that stretches back into the mists of time (that descend rather rapidly, as they do for most families in Britain).

Import and export

There are stories other than the decline and fall to be told about Britain; and since all nations *misrepresent* their past, I want to contribute to such misrepresentation by introducing a glimpse of my own sense of what Britishness has been. This is not only to throw into relief the partiality of what now passes for Britishness but also to set the imagination to work. As Benedict Anderson has suggested in *Imagined Communities*, all nations need to be imagined since only very few people who belong to a national community can possibly know one another.

Just for the moment imagine a Britain that has been a multi-ethnic state for a long time, has had an appreciable appetite for change (as well as for power) and has been in the import/export business for longer than anyone can remember, trading goods, materials, ideas – and building its Greatness by trading people as commercial property, and appropriating land and resources. There are signs of this import/export business everywhere and not merely in Britain's history of overseas market trading that stretches from sugar in the seventeenth century to the financial services of the present. Signs of Britain's promiscuity can be seen all around us in the streets, whether in the city of Edinburgh where Tony Blair's old college, Fettes College, is designed as a French chateau; in Blackpool where the Tower is a clone of the Eiffel Tower; in Edward Lutyens' First World War memorials that stand in both Leicester and Delhi; in the street names of West Belfast, just off the Falls Road: Lucknow Street, Kashmir Road and Cawnpore Street; or in Berlin where the new Reichstag will be built by the British architect Norman Foster.

There are further signs of Britain's outward-going character in the traffic of ideas that it has engaged in, whether between Enlightenment Edinburgh and continental Europe in the late eighteenth century or between the United States and Britain in the postwar period. The British monarchy, at least as much as any aspect of British society, has been profoundly shaped by the nation state's relationships with elsewhere: in the late nineteenth century it became a monarchy for the Empire; and more recently its unwillingness to modernise may be in part a consequence of its core role as part of the British tourist industry.

There are other signs of Britain's contribution to the import/export business, if more are needed, in the various communities from Britain that have been exported elsewhere and in the communities within Britain that have been imported from other countries. Chinese sailors arrived here to settle in the eighteenth century, a time at which, according to one account, a quarter of the British navy was black. During the same period, as the historian Linda Colley has recorded in her marvellous book *Britons*, the British of all classes travelled more than their European counterparts – something that seems to be a tradition since contemporary statistics suggest that the British are more emigrant minded within Europe than their western European neighbours. Even the scion of settledness, the mining community, moved from coalfield to coalfield, often pushed by necessity. It is an old Cornish joke that at the bottom of any mine in the world there will be a Cornish miner; and my own family moved from the South Wales through the Kent to the Yorkshire coalfield within two generations. The British fascination with home is precisely an index of how often the British have left it, not how little.

For such an outward-going nation, is it any wonder that its arts, both high and popular, have been washed by the sea. This is as true of Turner's 'slave ship' painting as it is of Paul McCartney's folksy 'The Mull of Kintyre' or the imperial 'Rule Britannia'; it's there in Shakespeare's *The Tempest* and in the BBC's *When the Boat Comes In*. And the popular British historical imagination until recently lived at sea, with Francis Drake and with the Scottish fishing fleet; with Bonnie Prince Charlie sailing over the sea to Skye and exile, and with the Welsh Prince Madoc's 'discovery' of America. This is, of course, not to say that the sea has a common meaning for those who live in Britain, that it is remembered or imagined in a uniform way – or that it is something simply to be celebrated. To take two testing examples: the sea should conjure up as part of British historical memory the boats on which the slaves were transported and the ships on which the persecuted Scottish Covenentors set sail to America. It is not primarily a question of admiring or damning this outward-looking Britain. But to *forget* this Britain in favour of a dream of cosy insularity is not to see Britain or its history at all.

If we were searching for an index of this place I have described, then the clothing (including fashion) industry might do. It is not merely that fashion and the clothing industry have been important elements of the national economic and cultural life for a long time, but that a casual glance at their history would show how they have been part of the traffic between here and elsewhere. The clothing industry was central to the relationship between the Caribbean and Britain and to the slave trade as early as the seventeenth century; fashion was important in the relationship between Britain and France in the next century when Frenchmen looked over the Channel to see what they should wear; cloth was again central in the nineteenth century when Manchester workers and Indian workers locked horns over cotton; in the 1930s, an English fashion designer was at the heart of Parisian haute couture; and more recently, whether through designers such as Vivienne Westwood or entrepreneurs such as Shami Ahmed, owner of the Manchester-based Joe Bloggs jeans, Britain's reputation in clothing and fashion is high. And this is of course not to mention Marks & Spencer, a chain of shops set up two men, one a member of the Russian Jewish community imported into Britain in the late nineteenth century. This 'immigrant' business is now a flagship of Britain across the world.

If reference to fashion in this imagining of the British seems wrongheaded, why is this? Is it because fashion is trivial? But is it any more so than football which is pored over as an index of the state of the national psyche? Perhaps fashion is just not manly enough to represent a nation that has been taught to pride itself on its manliness, whether in the Sandhurst mess, on the pitch at Cardiff Arms Park, the Manchester shop floor or the Glasgow pub? Or is it the fact that fashion and clothing offer back to the nation a vision of itself as a curious and outward-looking place, fascinated by change and display? If this does answer to some sense of Britain, is it any wonder that the dowdy buttoned-up civic culture of the Labour authorities in the 80s was dumped so readily by its supposed constituents when offered a brighter alternative?

Of course such a vision of an outward-looking nation in love with change simply cannot be accommodated in the current orthodoxy about the national psyche which, in most of its variants, is a tale of backward-looking insularity, melancholy decline and loss. Why is it now that Mary Quant's 60s version of British women – 'looking, listening, ready to try anything new' – seems so outlandish?

Perhaps it is by now such established wisdom that we are an insular old country that it comes as rather a shock to be reminded of what Mary Quant said. Or to read Elizabeth Bowen, the Irish novelist, as recently as 1942 commenting in *Seven Winters* thus on England, the supposed scion of antiquity: 'this newness of England, manifest in the brightness, occasionally the crudity of its colouring, had about it something of the precarious. Would it last?'

There *are* traditions of newness not only in England but in the whole of Britain – whether we look at the forging of technical innovations in watch and clock making during Charles II's reign, which as Angus Calder reminds us in *Revolutionary Empires*, was a 'prototype of all precise engineering'; Richard Branson's willingness to embark on new enterprises, from record producing to airlines and radio stations; the speed and appetite with which post Second World War women in Britain took up the 'new look', expressly frowned upon by a Labour Government believing that the rationing of the war needed to continue; the passion with which the young in Britain have taken to the emergent new multi-media technologies, all the way from the despised computer games to the Internet; or the traffic between American and Caribbean black music and British musicians. And of course the British appetite for the new does not stop at the doorstep of the home. The British house is now a haven for all things new, from computers to exercise equipment.

There have even been times in the past when whole new towns have been built to celebrate patriotism, such as was the case in the mid eighteenth century when the new town in Edinburgh was built to celebrate, in the historian Linda Colley's words, 'British patriotism... an assertion of Scotland's and the city's importance in the Union'. (A less curmudgeonly and more imaginative government might have seen the Channel Tunnel in not dissimilar terms.) And newness in Britain is not necessarily opposed to tradition: the green concerns that are characteristic of the new politics renew traditional British concerns with this green and pleasant land.

It is not, then, that the new is antithetical to the British – only to certain powerful elements, often within the left. For instance, to read the description in George Orwell's novel *Coming Up for Air* of the hero eating an American style frankfurter – 'bombs of filth [explode] inside your mouth' – is to hear an authentic voice of the left which loathes both newness and foreignness. (You don't have to like frankfurters to make this judgement on Orwell.) And it is worth remembering that the 30s and 40s British passion for America, against which Orwell was reacting, was fuelled not only by a desire for frivolous novelties but, as Mass Observation found out during the Second World War, by the British people's admiration for America's democracy.

To hear the contemporary version of Orwell is to listen to Tony Benn, after the 1983 election, saying on television that the election was lost for Labour by the people who had opted to have Georgian doors fitted to their houses (that is, the people who had bought their council houses). He spoke more profoundly than he knew. Not only did he reveal that revulsion against change that has so scarred parts of the Labour Movement but he implicitly realised – while loathing it – that the Georgian doors were a sign of modernisation, not some refuge in heritage. The historian Raphael Samuel has argued in his recent *Theatres of Memory* that the British passion for DIY, even the passion for period effects, should be seen as a form of modernisation. Yet if this is the case, why the cries against it? Part of the explanation, according to Samuel, is that the drapes and other Georgian effects, so fashionable at present, are very feminine, so unlike the last moment of domestic modernisation in Britain in the 50s, which was very masculine, with its flushed doors, hard edges and straight lines.

It is profitable to push this further and suggest that the masculinity to which the British have held so strongly – identifying themselves as such against the 'effeminate' French or the feminine Asians – may be changing messily, unevenly and with great resistance into a more feminine identity. If this is the case, then it is hardly surprising that it is experienced as a crisis by some, since to be unmanly *and* British has for such a long time been worse than a crime that 'effeminacy' is reached for as a term of abuse in the most unlikely circumstances. When the republican radical Tom Paine wanted to damn the unpatriotic British aristocracy in the late eighteenth century, he did so by calling it a 'seraglio of males'. And of course more recently, in the high period of British imperialism, the core subject of the Public Schools was the conjunction of patriotism and masculinity. Even Protestantism, the chosen historical religion of the British has been seen as a truly manly religion, so unlike that effete Catholicism – a view that echoes from Charles Kingsley as he denounced the unmanly Catholic convert JH Newman down to Ian Paisley as he fulminates against the 'Whore of Rome'. Yet wherever the British look at present, they see the old schoolrooms of masculinity under siege – the pub under pressure from the cafe; the Spion Kop of the football ground giving way to seats and family enclosures, and masculine manufacturing industry losing out to feminine service industries such as tourism.

The Royal Family has been the place where this contest between a traditional British masculinity and a new modernising femininity has been most outrageously staged, in the battle between Prince Charles and Princess Diana. The renewed discussion of the role of the Monarchy in the constitutional life of the nation – Mr Major recently called it with his usual grace, the 'glue' – may well be the consequence of its failure in the moral sphere, where it had actually gained its authority. The discussions about the future of the Monarchy are a sign that it is effectively finished. The mistreatment of Princess Diana by what Beatrix Campbell called in *The Guardian* an 'authoritarian, selfish, whimsical, conservative patriarch' has damaged the monarchy in the public's eyes much more than the masculine constitutional arguments of groups such as Charter 88 – and perhaps mortally so. It also confirmed that reimagining Britain and transforming masculinity may not be a million miles apart, something that is hardly touched on by the political parties at all.

Of course there is no virtue in modernisation in and for itself, although there may be virtue in nurturing a curious spirit. But nor is there any necessary virtue in tradition. When only a few years ago the marketing manager of Robertson's jam could respond to the attacks on his company's use of the golliwog by saying 'Golly is part of our national tradition. An attack on it is an attack on part of British culture', the limited value of an appeal to tradition ought to have been clear enough. It's also the case that even if certain things are not traditional – even when claimed to be – they may still be valuable. Certainly the early nineteenth-century British would have been amused to hear that they were kind to animals. But that does not diminish the value of the actions of those who at present are trying to stop the trade in animals across Europe.

The simple fact is that the British have to *choose* their values, make their allegiances and loyalties rather than genuflect before – or simply try to pull down – tradition.

Pure lust

The political administrations of Mrs Thatcher are vital in this regard since at the same time they fixed Britishness as their keystone, they claimed to reconcile newness with tradition. It was not merely that her ambition was to stop Britain being a nation in retreat (which incoming Prime Minister has not said that) but that she had a new story to tell about Britain and Britishness, a story, she claimed, which was actually an ancient one that the more recent ones had simply obliterated. Put simply, Britain was a special place, beset now as of old, by enemies within and without, but possessed of a destiny that could never be thwarted. One might say that part of the tension between the Queen and the Government during Mrs Thatcher's regimes was due to the fact that the National Story the Prime Minister told was more compelling than the one held in trust by the Monarchy – which had offered itself as The Family in a land of families, indeed as the head of an inclusive family to which all the nations of these islands (plus the Commonwealth) might belong.

Mrs Thatcher's Britishness depended rather on a sustained process of *purification* and *exclusion*. In her British story, enemies were here, there and everywhere.

Britishness was singular, not plural and it was enough to be one of 'them' by not being 'one of us'. Mrs Thatcher hardly invented such a strategy since Britishness has long worked on the principle of separating the inside sheep from the outside goats. Sometimes they have been Catholics, denied the vote, other times they have been Jewish people, and more recently people from the Caribbean or Asia. While the groups may change, the principle does not – their presence threatens the historic identity of the British. It is not as if such rallying cries around purification have gone away entirely – look at a speech by Michael Portillo or Charles Wardle's recent 'immigration scaremongering' for contrary evidence. But it does seem to be the case that they are no longer always capable of providing an Island Story to which enough are willing to subscribe.

Mrs Thatcher was not the first to work in terms of insiders and outsiders, nor the first to look on the British (and perhaps particularly the English) as a people with a special destiny. After all it was as long ago as 1500 that an Italian visitor said that 'they think that there are no other men than themselves and no other world than England'. There are many explanations for the sense of superiority that the British, and particularly the English, have historically felt towards other nations and foreigners in general. Linda Colley has been persuasive in demonstrating how important Protestantism was in the eighteenth century in helping to unify the various ethnic groups within Britain by marking them out from others, in Europe and elsewhere. At the core of this eighteenth century Britishness was the sense of a destiny-driven militant (and where necessary military) Protestant people surrounded by a hostile Catholic Europe, and threatened by dangerous colonies from without and various enemies from within (whether Scottish nationalists or aristocratic renegade cosmopolitans).

Of course the importance of Protestantism goes back earlier than the period with which Linda Colley's book is concerned. The Italian visitor of 1500 said what he did on the eve of England's break with Rome, at the moment when the English King took final responsibility for his subjects' religious spiritual safety as much as their physical, an event which effectively made England the principal Protestant power in Europe. When Mrs Thatcher started setting about the Civil Service, it was hard not to remember the closing down of the monasteries during Henry VIII's reign, when in the mid 1530s, around 9000 nuns and monks were sent out into the world. Most of them received generous pensions, although around a quarter did not.

It might even be said that Thatcher was the last leader of that Protestant Britishness which saw itself as the guardian of the light in the darkness – she was a Methodist and was prone to speak of Britons. As she phrased it herself in 1984, during the Miners' Strike: "We had to fight an enemy without in the Falklands. We always have to be aware of the enemy within, which is more difficult and dangerous to liberty". With Mrs Thatcher, liberty was the standard around which the British people were asked to quell the enemy within, the working-class miners, as much as the enemy without, General Galtieri. Thatcher's strength was the capacity not simply to appeal to some already constituted sense of Britishness – any more than the patriots of the eighteenth century simply subscribed to some already existing Britishness – but to orchestrate elements of the national life and history, often contradictory ones, and help them make persuasive sense in her story.

The enemies may have been legion – miners, the EC, Galtieri, the wets in her own party – but what allowed her to identify the enemies within as enemies, as much as the enemies without, was their betrayal of the British whose spokeswoman she declared herself to be. Some of her enemies were characterised as importers of unBritish beliefs such as socialism; some groups were said to have put their own, often professional, interests before Britain's: a medley of groups including schoolteachers and civil servants fell into this category; others, it was claimed, universalised their own sectional tastes and imposed them on the British: the Arts Council and trendy BBC types were among the examples. Yet others, recently settled here, threatened to import alien cultures that would swamp Britain's historic one.

Sometimes she could draw on political traditions within the national culture to combat her enemies: a National Theatre funded by the state is 'alien to the spirit of our nation' and 'individual effort and personal competition are a healthier stimulus than the motherly or grandmotherly feelings of a state nurse', said Sir Charles Wyndham in apparently unmistakeable Thatcherite tones, in *The Daily Telegraph* of 1908. With other 'enemies' she could draw on what has been a popular British mistrust of the state's servants. With yet others she could draw on a history of the People's resentment against ancient vested interests – when she took on, say, the legal profession or the Universities or even the Trades Unions (the union bosses always identified as 'them' against the union members who were 'us'). At one moment she drew on what has come to be known as a Churchillian rhetoric during the Falklands War; at another, on a Powellite language of race, which has deep roots within an old imperial power. And of course in 1984 during the conflict with the miners, she drew ruthlessly on the coercive powers of the state.

Thatcher no more wanted to return to Victorian values than the French revolutionaries of 1789 wanted to return to the Roman republic which they feted. Each dressed themselves in old clothes in order to modernise their respective countries and identities. To do this, Mrs Thatcher first had to disable the traditional sources of authority who claimed to represent Britain and to incarnate Britishness.

Harold Perkin in his marvellous synoptic study, *The Rise of the Professional Society*, has pointed out that the twentieth century is the century not of the common man or woman, but of the expert. And although he does not say this, it may be the case with national identity as with much else: the arguments have been primarily among elites. One way of defining British intellectuals in the postwar period might be to say that they have claimed property rights over national identity – EP Thompson and his radical People versus Tom Nairn, with his unmodernised British state; Alan Macfarlane, with his 'discovery' that the English were individualists as early as the medieval period versus the High Anglican Burkean Britishness of Roger Scruton.

Certainly Thatcher defined and identified her own populist Britishness in opposition to an elite one. (The People were her song as much as they had been the song of the left at earlier times: 'Trust the people', was her cry.) She wanted to imagine, in her own words, 'days of hope', 'not hopelessness' and often struck a warlike pose, not unattractive to a nation whose identity has often been remade through war: 'We are witnessing a deliberate attack on our values... a deliberate attack on our heritage and our great past. And there are those who gnaw away at our national self-respect, rewriting British history as centuries of unrelieved gloom, oppression and failure'. Against all Britain's foes, without and within, there had to be a call to arms. 'There is no week, nor day, nor hour when tyranny may not enter upon this country, if the people lose their supreme confidence in themselves, and lose their roughness and spirit of defiance. Tyranny may always enter – there is no charm or bar against it'.

Roughness is an interesting term to use of the British people. It is certainly far from that English Home Counties version which flatters them by describing them in Orwell's terms as a quiet, peaceable people. And roughness in Thatcher's version does seem to carry a class connotation when it is explicitly opposed to charm. The venom with which the elite responded to her 'roughness' showed how thin the veneer of charm could be. Baroness Mary Warnock is reported in Hugo Young's biography, *One of Us*, as seeing the Prime Minister shopping at Marks & Spencer and being driven to declare that the clothes showed a woman 'packaged together in a way that's not exactly vulgar, just low'. Who said that clothes don't matter to the British?

Even if it were possible to draw up a balance sheet on the two contending ideas of Britishness, that struggled in the 80s and in the ruins of which we now live, this would not be the place to do it. But it may be worth suggesting how they operated in one sector, the arts. For elite Britain whose brainchild the 1946 Arts Council was, culture was good for you: the arts were part of the national interest. As recently as the 1960s, Lord Goodman said that a dose of culture could turn hooligans into citizens.

The arts, in short, were the cultural version of the welfare state milk that was given to all school children: the arts nourished the mind as the milk the bones. As real and valuable as the achievements of this welfare state culture were (I was one of its beneficiaries as a working class grammar school educated child), there were major deficiencies built into its assumptions. This was a world where everything had its place. The fine arts (the Arts Council's responsibility) were separated from the popular ones and enjoyed the vast majority of the grants; (English) metropolitan standards were the touchstone against which all else was judged; the various boards worked by patronage and were answerable to their peers rather than a wider constituency; the substantive part of the grant was devoted to minority metropolitan based arts; there was indifference to new practitioners in order to disseminate the best arts from the past; and there was a staggering indifference to recent arts and to new technologies, where the received distinctions between commerce and culture were blurred.

Although this indifference was not something with which Mrs Thatcher charged the elite, it ought to have been, since what was in part important and culturally innovative about Britain during the Lord Goodman arts-are-good-for-you period was the world of rock-n-roll, wholly unsponsored by the state, which helped to transform all the other arts, from British film to British art, became an important British export and is now as important a part of the British heritage as anything else.

Mrs Thatcher's strategy, with the arts as with much else, was to appeal over the head of the elite to the British people. Thatcher identified 'them' as not 'one of us' and wanted to know why 'their' tastes were imposed on and paid for by the majority; why the arts 'ran down' Britain; and why the arts should enjoy protected status? When Norman Tebbit asked why it was wrong to look at Page 3 Girls since the elite went into art galleries to look at paintings of nudes, he seemed to be parodying radical cultural critics' earlier attacks on high culture.

In her fight against the 'Establishment', Mrs Thatcher had a comrade in arms in Rupert Murdoch. Through the setting up of *Sky* as much as through *The Sun*, Murdoch played a vigorous part in mocking and abusing the elite's tastes and power, promising his viewers and readers fun rather than enlightenment and offering choice rather than instruction. Like Mrs Thatcher, Murdoch was adept at using language that bit deep into British history. 'The freeing of broadcasting in this country', he said at the Edinburgh Television Festival, 'is very much part of [the] democratic revolution, and an essential step forward into the Information Age.' How would an audience of television executives brought up to believe that they were the guardians of British freedom and democracy respond when someone such as Murdoch stole their clothes? The truth is, as William Shawcross observes in his biography of Murdoch, they didn't effectively demur. Their silence was tantamount admission that they knew *their* Britain and the top-down Reithianism they had inherited were dead and that they could not imagine a future other than the consumerist one Murdoch offered them. It was another sign that a further keystone in the postwar settlement had crashed. The tragedy was that Murdoch and Thatcher's aggressive populism was not unanswerable; it was simply that the elite who controlled the arts including broadcasting in Britain had become so inturned that it had never had to justify itself to anyone who did not share its convictions or whom it could not simply dismiss as 'low'.

British professionals – all the way from arts administrators to health professionals – are still traumatised by what happened in the 80s, and on the whole have failed to regroup and understand that they have to find a way of talking with and to people rather than, as traditionally, for them. Nowhere has this been clearer than in higher education where massification has taken place against the wishes of the profession, who on the whole had been happy to talk endlessly about excluded and marginalised groups, on the understanding that they did not have to teach them. Of course it may well be, as Harold Perkin has argued, that the Thatcherite project was never seriously committed to the popular and that her regime actually was a struggle between the old professions and the new managerial ones. And certainly looking at the new regimes that are installed in the Universities, it is difficult to feel more tender towards this managerial elite than towards those that preceded it. But even if Perkin's analysis is correct, it still remains the case that, against the elite Britishness that saw the country as decent, tolerant, settled, and nonmaterialistic, and in which certain groups were deputised to speak on its behalf, Thatcher orchestrated a different Britain and Britishness. It was intolerant both of privilege (the Royal Family) and of difference (British culture swamped by 'alien' cultures); it had an appetite for unsanctioned ambitions (as Thomas Hardy said, given the choice between luxury and culture, the poor will often choose luxury first); it wasn't quiet and kind to animals but capable of fierce and warlike feeling; and it was far from happy to know its place but rather noisy and undeferential and pleasure-seeking. What the Thatcher years proved was that Britishness wasn't simply out there waiting to be called into action but was a potential that could have a whole host of meanings.

English intimacies

If Thatcher's regimes tried to *settle* Britain, the project of the day ought now to be to *unsettle* it – to keep open a range of meanings around Britishness. What it is to be British ought always to be plural, not singular as Mrs Thatcher contended: heterogeneous rather than pure; incomplete rather than monumentally finished. This is not simply ethically preferable to the Keep Britain Pure campaign that Mrs Thatcher ran; it also answers more adequately to the country's history as well as to Britain's present needs where a willingness to embrace heterogeneity as a resource rather than reject it as dilution, is likely to be key to the country's political, economic and cultural survival.

At one level the proposal to accept a heterogeneous Britain ought to be uncontentious since this nation state is made up of three countries (or do I mean four, including Northern Ireland, or do I mean Ulster?), and so in the most obvious sense has lived with multiple affiliations and loyalties for a very long time. So settled is this settled country, in fact, that it doesn't even have a settled name. It's certainly arguable that its variety of names is simply a symptom of something else: that there isn't even agreement about what the nation-state is to be identified with: the monarch (United Kingdom), the people (Scottish, Welsh etc) or the systems of government? The passport may well say British – and of course Great Britain was effectively founded after the Battle of Culloden, in 1707. But since 1800 it has been more accurate, if in practice unusual, to call the country the United Kingdom of Great Britain and Ireland (and after 1921, this became Northern Ireland). But to do this leaves us with a country around the same age as the United States of America, an unsettling thought when the orthodox stories about Britain rattle on about how old this country is. And anyway, how many of the British say that they are from the UK?

Whatever the anxieties generated by present reflections on national identity, not the least of the opportunities the present moment offers is the opportunity to flush out the English – for among the nations of this island it is they who have been most reluctant to come face to face. When, around twenty years ago, the poet CH Sisson wrote in *Poetry Nation* that 'The English are at present mercifully free from the duty which appears to weigh upon the Scots, Irish and Welsh, of talking as if they were themselves', he spoke a commonsense that has now passed away. But the trauma for the English of speaking 'as if they were themselves' should not be underestimated. After all, it is an awkward feeling for someone who has put others under the spotlight to find themselves the specimen for examination.

It may well be that it is the intimate yet superior way in which the English have lived with so many other groups that has allowed them not to think about themselves. English slides so easily into British – whether in the case of the BBC where there is a BBC Scotland but no BBC England; or at crucial historical moments such as 1939 when a certain politician was invited to 'speak for England' or in 1866, when Disraeli could say at the height of the British Empire, that 'no power... interferes more than England. She interferes in Asia because she is really more of an Asiatic Power than a European'. When the

Daily Mail demands that Private Clegg as an Englishman should have had access to British justice in the form of a jury trial but does not go on to extend it to others tried in the Diplock courts in Northern Ireland, it is only doing what the English have often done: claim for themselves rights they don't feel the rest of the United Kingdom (never mind anywhere else) deserve. This has been going on for a long time, at least since the Welsh, in the words of historian Gwyn Williams, were turned into 'unpersons without civil rights' during Glyn Dŵr's rebellion.

The underbelly of the English sense of superiority to all and sundry, of course, has been a terror of its inferiority, as one can witness in the eighteenth century when the success of the Scots in England led to an English anxiety about the Scots' sexual potency. *Plus ça change*, as the English say.

But it is not merely that the English have repressed their intercourse with other nations and groups, they have considered themselves to be an inviolate People: a self-generated homogenous community, driven by a special destiny. As the historian Raphael Samuel put it in the *New Left Review*, not talking of Mrs Thatcher but he might have been: for the left 'the English people have somehow been singled out for a place in history... the English language is superior to others, and... the liberty of the individual is more secure in England than it is abroad'. In George Orwell's *The Lion and the Unicorn*, his hymn to patriotism written during the Second World War, he could write of the homogenous community that England was. And it took Cairns Craig, a recent Scottish writer to point out of EP Thompson's classic study *The Making of the English Working Class* that its unwillingness to address Scottish or Welsh history allowed him to maintain the fantasy that English working-class history could be talked of without reference to elsewhere.

If one response to English nationalism has been to see the potential of radical patriotism, another has been an obvious and studied distaste. For this group Englishness means the Last Night of the Proms, Rule Britannia, and at the far end of the corridor, the British National Party and the neo-fascists who recently waved the flag and waged war in Dublin. But distaste isn't good enough.

The need for the English to come face to face was never clearer than in the report over the killing of Ahmed Ullah, the English Asian boy by the white English boy in 1986 in the Burnage school in Manchester. The report on the killing mentioned that of all the groups in the school, the white English working class children had the least sense of who they were. It may well be uncomfortable for the white English to have to consider themselves an ethnic group, but that's what they are. The received visions, whether of the upper-middle-class-stiff-upper-lip-but-full-of-deep-feeling male, or of the male-working-class-breadwinner-looking-after-his-family-in-a-settled-community are no longer functional and simply can't answer, and never have, to the range of English experience that has been available. How can such an iconography accommodate popular English figures such as the northern gay bleached blond painter David Hockney; the 'Essex girl' and captain of the British women's athletic team Sally Gunnell; the public school former rock music entrepreneur Richard Branson; or the London-based music producer and entrepreneur Jazzy B?

One response to the crisis of self-scrutiny among the white English has been to bury England, with full ceremonial honours, five fathoms deep. This appears to have been the recommendation of David Starkey whose article in *The Guardian*, as I have said, is such a gem: 'England, like that other great Empire of Rome, is dead', says Starkey. 'Like Rome, it survives as a legal system and a literature. It has become a place of the mind.'

The virtues of this position for the necrophiliac are clear: it ensures that England is not subject to change and can be lovingly watered and maintained in the privacy of one's own mind. (It goes without saying that the death of England is one of the things the English have loved announcing for hundreds of years.) While it is fascinating to see the lengths some people will go to protect the purity and changelessness of the loved object, the truth is that England has never been pure – and that is something the white English profoundly need to understand, if they are to stop seeing every offer of a new relationship – from the new English to Europe – as a threat to their integrity and homogeneity. Too often, it appears as if the two alternatives are to be English or to be cosmopolitan, that is, to belong to England or to belong to the world – whereas there are many ways of belonging to the world.

After all, how far would you have to go back to pinpoint a prelapsarian England, before it had knowledge of other places? The vision of the English as a nation of gardeners and country lovers has its roots in England's relationships with other countries. As the historian Alun Howkins has argued, the modern invention of England as an essentially rural place is born in the imagination of an urban England in the late nineteenth century, intensely anxious about the effects on Britain's competitive and imperial power of the flight from the land and of the debilitation of urban life. Even the origins of the icon of domestic Englishness, the greenhouse, are anything but domestic. The greenhouse was invented to be able to maintain and study fauna brought back from colonial countries. And more recently, there is a pleasant irony in the fact that the late James Herriot who has given fresh identity to the Yorkshire Dales was a Scotsman. To say all this is far from saying that the origins of these English pleasures necessarily impugns their importance – as I have said before, traditional or not, it is their value to us now we have to judge – but it is to say that they cannot be used to buttress the claim that the English are a self-enclosed people.

But such claims are still lamentably far from rare. 'British Society between the two world wars was peculiarly inward looking', claims the historian, Raphael Samuel. But was that the case, even in England, whether the 'S' is upper or lower case? Where is the evidence, even in the cultural sphere? Is it there in the last words of George V, which were 'How is the Empire?'; or in those icons of English art, John Piper and Henry Moore, who were engaged with European surrealism in the 30s; or in English writers whose metaphors were of travel and movement (Graham Greene's *Stamboul Train*) and who were themselves always on the move; or in the English cinema of that central European migrant to England, Alexander Korda whose epic films for Rank included *The Four Feathers* (about the Sudanese wars of the late nineteenth century) and *Henry VIII*; or in post franchise women's fashion which looked across the channel; or the dance band craze, drawing on black and white American musical models, which swept places from the Savoy Hotel, London to the BBC which invited listeners to 'Roll up the carpet and dance'; or in the popular appetite for tinned food (an eagerly received import from the States)? Even Daphne Du Maurier's hymn to English domesticity, *Rebecca*, is haunted by a life in Monte Carlo and by a sexual imagination that finds expression in profoundly racial terms.

If the black English in the postwar period have been drawing on resources outside Britain as well as within in helping to forge new Englands, they have been doing, within particular networks and with quite extraordinary achievements, little different from what earlier English formations, with other networks, had done before them. It has simply been racism that has stigmatised black English networks as 'other' and has repressed the promiscuity of the white English. John Constable doesn't become less English because he engaged in a dialogue with European landscape painting any more than does Hanif Kureishi because part of his imagination is engaged with the Indian subcontinent.

It is of course clear that the historical promiscuity of the white English can coexist with a contempt for others – and that is the case whether the examples are the poet Philip Larkin whose love of the jazz of Louis Armstrong and Sidney Bechet coexisted happily with an ugly racism or the teddy boys of the 50s whose love of black-derived rock'n'roll did not stop them precipitating the Notting Hill riots. The tragedy of the moment is that no-one in positions of effective power is willing to turn the mixing and matching that has been the experience of all the English into a coherent political story that would help them to understand their differences and their commonality. It is no use politicians appealing to an English community as if it were already constituted. It is precisely that community that needs to be imagined.

In praise of mongrels

What is needed now, then, not only in relationship to England but also with the whole of Britain, is a way of thinking about national identity that recognises the extraordinary diversity, past and present, within the islands without making the mistake of thinking that Britain is made up of a series of archipelagos. The danger of this 'archipelagoisation' is most clear in 'racial' terms where the equation of Britishness and whiteness, which Mrs Thatcher's governments nourished in the 80s, has led certain black groups to adopt their own Keep Black Pure line, most notably the British Muslims who opposed Salman Rushdie. But in political terms such Muslims are only the mirror image of the right-wing thinker John Casey who said recently in the *Sunday Telegraph* that the problems with Islam 'arise from Western ideas imported into the Muslim world'. Both sides of the fundamentalist coin want to resist the import/export culture, which has been going on for centuries and retain fantasies of virginity. But dreams of purity also arise in more surprising quarters. In a review in *The Guardian* of a recent biography of Tony Blair, Michael Foot said Cherie Blair was 'pure English working class' before he remembered she was partly Irish. Against all such dreams of purity – whether of class, culture or nation – we need to insist upon the historical experience of interpenetration. Caribbean Welshness or Asian Scottishness is no more a contradiction – despite what the recent Census would lead you to believe – than any of the many combinations that are possible within Britain.

No one should underestimate that the claim to be British has certain rights attached to it, something too easily taken for granted by those who have had its protection for a long time. It was a Welshman who first coined the term 'The British Empire' in the sixteenth century precisely so that England could not keep the riches for itself. The virtues of being British were equally clear to a Yorkshire-Asian girl opposed to Rushdie who said in 1989 that she was weary of being told to behave in Rome as the Romans: she was a Roman, she said. In other words, a *Muslim Briton* who refused to be made to choose between two of her identities, demanding to have both recognised.

But given what is happening in Europe, the impulse towards a radical simplification and towards separation in Britain may be strong – along ethnic and national lines. Where such an impulse seems most strong at present is in Scotland, not surprisingly, given the gap between the political make-up of Scotland and Westminster. It's possible to imagine someone saying, 'Let's start by simply shuffling off British identity' and going on to demand that the four countries are separated out: England, (Northern) Ireland, Scotland, Wales. The attractions of this are obvious and it would at least allow the possibility of recognising the complexity that lies behind the term Britain. And there are certainly histories that can be called Scottish or Welsh histories that cannot be swallowed up in what has passed for British history and ought not to pass as footnotes to English history – as did Wales in the 1911 *Encyclopaedia Britannica*, where, under the entry Wales, it simply said 'see England'. And of course there are problems that are peculiar to each of the countries. If it is the Tory Party in England in the 90s that has been subject to accusations of sleaze, the culprit in Scotland has been the Labour Party, at Monklands – something difficult to blame on the English.

It may be that Tam Dalyell is right and it is either the Union or independence – there is no middle way – and that the people of these countries will in the long term choose the latter. But if they do, problems over national identity won't simply go away. First, the problem of definition isn't evaded by replacing Britishness with, say, Scottishness, if the belief is that the latter is transparent. As numerous commentators have said there is at least as much heterogeneity within Scotland as there is between Scotland and England; and as Gwyn Williams has argued eloquently in *When Was Wales?*, the North Wales Welsh have been historically reluctant to acknowledge the English-speaking people of the industrialised South as Welsh, and have been happier to talk of them as British or even, the worst insult, as English. This is clear at a popular level every time that professional Welsh writer Jan Morris speaks of the Welsh in terms of the language.

It may well be that there are, as Settlerwatch who seem to wish to expel the English from Scotland claim, problems of the power of the English within Scotland, but what is important is that these problems are not formulated in terms of purity or impurity. It simply ought to be too late in history for that.

This is a mongrel island and the people who make up the populations of the countries here have historically been mongrels. As Victor Kiernan, an historian has said, the British are 'clearly among the most ethnically composite of the Europeans'. One of the problems with the Labour Party's proposals over English regional government is that this may promote a belief that there is, say, an unproblematic English northern identity, just as pure and uncontaminated as English or British national identity is still sometimes said to be. There isn't. There never was, and there will never be. Insofar as these traditional regional identities have been assumed and appealed to, they have often worked in terms of exclusion, whether one thinks of Yorkshire Cricket Club's refusal to employ Asian Yorkshire cricketers or the racism that the Newcastle footballer Andy Cole and his family faced in the north-east. And, in any case, as we northerners are wont to say, which Northernness are we to choose? Is it the Northernness captured in the 'gritty films' of the 60s, the outcome of a miscegenated relationship between northern scholarship boys and gay southern filmmakers? Or the north of historians such as EP Thompson who have sung of its radical settledness? Or is it the northernness that broke into visibility in the early 60s, as Thompson published his book, a northernness with an appetite for the new, nourished both by the music scene for which the Beatles will do as shorthand and by the dirty dealings of John Poulson and T Dan Smith who imagined a new Newcastle?

The second problem set up by the separatist position, which believes that smaller units are more clear cut, is that it simply won't face up to how intimately the countries that have made up Britain have been involved. While this could be shown by looking at the complex legal relationships among the countries, it is more visible and emotionally entangled in the field of sport. It isn't as if even on the sportsfield our loyalties are settled. For instance in football there are four countries including Northern Ireland, while in Rugby Union there are four 'home' countries (including the whole of Ireland) who play together overseas as the British Lions; in Athletics there is the Great Britain team as there is in Rugby League even though the majority of players in the latter are drawn from a couple of counties in the north of England. Such is the complexity of the history, then, that if we are to move beyond the current version of Britishness – which is often a smokescreen for Englishness – it can only be done by going forward.

Of course, part of the attraction of 'Europe' among some of the Scots and Welsh (as well as some of the English) is that it can apparently offer a way out from under a Great Britain dominated by the English.

The Welsh can become through a hyphen Welsh-Europeans, the Scots, Scots-Europeans and so on. But repentance is unlike innocence as my Methodist teachers taught me, and there is no way back for any of the countries that make up the United Kingdom of Great Britain and Northern Ireland to some pristine uncontaminated identity before the weddings – which in some cases were certainly shotgun.

It may be the case that Europe does offer great opportunities for the various nations that make up Britain, but joining Europe will resolve nothing, if the British use it as a moment to postpone once again having to come face to face. For to come face to face involves not only facing up to each of the historical identities of the countries that make up these islands in relationship with each other, and in relationship with Europe but also in relationship to the countries which once made up the empire and whose histories and those of the British are as tied as those of siamese twins. Sometimes the lust after Europe can seem just another excuse for amnesia about the historical connections of the British with other parts of the globe: from America to Hong Kong, from Jamaica to India. The question is, can Britain recognise this and reinvent itself and at the same time slough off the profound habit of rule and superiority which has been part of its history?

In the next century national identity will not exhaust the wider affiliations and loyalties that people will wish to commit themselves to within these islands. It does not exhaust them now. Some of these identities are familial, some local; some may be global; some are built around gender and others around generation. But among the available identities are – and will remain for the foreseeable future – national ones. What is needed now are identities in Britain that do not have to be thought of as either a badge of pride or shame. When Raymond Illingworth, the chairman of selectors of the English cricket team, said of England's lamentable performance in the recent Ashes in Australia, that the captain Michael

Atherton's responsibility was to 'Gee them [the players] up', he sounds as if being English is a question of the driver getting the horses to work a little better.

Being British (or for that matter being Scottish or Welsh or English) needs rather to be something you see is in your interest and something you want. Of course to propose a utilitarian version of national identity, one that is sufficiently flexible to allow numerous groups to have an interest and pleasure in subscribing to, may seem in poor taste. But it is precisely how Linda Colley speaks of the British national identity forged in the eighteenth century – it was something not inherited but learned, and something in the interest of the variety of ethnic groups to learn. Is it now possible to make Britishness a sufficiently attractive and usable identity that people would wish to subscribe to? If it isn't, it does not deserve our attention. If it is, then a critical issue would have to be the recognition that being British does not mean that you have to abandon other loyalties. After all, that was not the case in the past. British national identity in the eighteenth century was an identity that did not demand the annulment of other loyalties. Professor Colley makes this clear throughout her book, nowhere more so than when she writes that Iolo Morganwg, the late eighteenth century radical writer, could unhesitatingly say that Welsh was one of his two native tongues.

It is that recognition of the possibilities and pleasures of multiple belonging that we need to engender – in order that we can see how foolish was Norman Tebbit's claim that a single decision, the team for which you cheer, of all things, is the litmus paper of your identity and loyalty. This seems to be a very difficult lesson to learn in Britain, although given the heterogeneous mix of peoples and histories that have nourished the history of the present British people, it ought not to be. It may even be the case, hard though it is for many of the British to acknowledge, that they can learn from the Irish: for what is happening there could prefigure what might happen in Britain. After all it looks as if Ireland is launching itself on an experiment to see whether political and cultural diversity necessarily leads to conflict – and it is such diversity that is precisely what any usable and defensible British national identity would need to sustain and nurture.

This seems to be well understood by English Unionists such as Matthew D'Ancona who selectively leaked the Westminster/Dublin proposals in *The Times* and who has said – in appalled tones – that what is happening in Ireland may have profound consequences for the rest of the United Kingdom. Let us hope that he is right!

But no one should pretend that learning to live with difference and diversity will be easy. The furore that followed the decision by the Protestant-dominated Queen's University Belfast to abandon the national anthem at its graduation ceremonies to promote a neutral atmosphere for all its members is simply a local sign of the arguments to come. But the Joint Framework Document does give hope.

Northern Ireland will effectively have a bill of rights covering matters from the political to the cultural and the promise of a jurisdiction that must work impartially 'on behalf of all the people in Northern Ireland in their diversity'. And in his Commons statement Mr Major declared that he wanted to see 'institutions that reflect the different traditions in a manner acceptable to all'. Despite his rider that Northern Ireland is a 'special case' within the United Kingdom, it is clear that the political recognition of the legitimacy of difference and of multiple affiliations in one part of the United Kingdom will open up the way for the rest of us.

Millennium notes

The opportunities to reinvent the British are legion, particularly as the debates around the millennium celebrations intensify. The opportunities are certainly there for the 'old' nationalising institutions – such as the Tate Gallery, the BBC and the universities. For example, when the Tate establishes the museum of modern art at Bankside and gives over the Tate at Millbank to British art, how will it tell Our Story? Will it be as one single and settled Whig-like history in which English painting is called British painting and Scottish painting Scottish, where British art is kept unspotted from the world, where white European migrants here are viewed as British, while black migrant artists belong to another story? Or will the Gallery set up Our Story as a series of diverse, overlapping and sometimes clashing stories, at the core of which is the vision of British art as a promiscuous art, involved in the import/export business, with the Dieppe-living Sickert looking at Edgar Degas and the German migrant to England Frank Auerbach going on to reimagine the Camden Town of Sickert through the example of Giacometti and French existentialism. Will it invite curators beyond the professional caste to curate major parts of that history –

writers, filmmakers and even artists. Such a way of imagining British art would take the sometimes vexacious complexities of Britain's history and make of them an opportunity. Of course this assumes that argument and disagreement is not somehow 'unEnglish' or 'unBritish' and that we don't all prefer to return to a quiet consensual Britain where someone else always knows best. The evidence is that we don't.

Everywhere there are signs that the DIY British culture has stretched beyond Sainsbury's Homebase. It is there in the booming world of self-help and voluntary associations which demonstrate that the British distrust of politicians must not be confused with a withdrawal from public life; it is equally there in the passion for camcorders with which people record their own family history: it's there in the commitment to direct action politics; it's in the car boot sales that are part of the thriving black economy, partly a result of unemployment, but also an indication of the British love for buying and selling; it also remains a powerful impulse in the music industry where 'do-it-yourself' labels continue to rise, evaporate and fall. It's even there in the old British institutions such as the BBC whose *VideoNation* project, for all its archness, allows a wide range of people access to the new technologies enabling them to shape and imagine their own stories.

Such British in all their 57 varieties are not going to allow others to make judgements for them – to tell them who they are or what shape their national identity should take. They want to make their choice – to use one of Thatcher's keywords of the 80s. This won't make for restful days and nights, even in that bolthole of the politician's mind, 'middle England'. This is going to become a more, not less, turbulent place, as Britain renegotiates its life with itself and with others, in an increasingly globalised world. It won't be like a Grantchester tea-party but the majority of the British have never bought into that myth; they've simply not been offered anything else. What this Britain will need –

among much else – is politicians who are willing to enter this turbulence and find ways of telling national stories that are inclusive and open ended.

But these stories are going to be told in a world, as we all know, increasingly shaped by technologies that are effectively global, where the defining and most powerful images of national identity are likely to be on one form of screen or another and where knowledge will increasingly be found in electronic form.

At this point, a melancholic sigh about a new global homogenisation and the death of national cultures is usually expected and often provided. Or there are jokes about the British lion being tamed by the computer mouse. But what if this technology is seen as an opportunity rather than a deadly virus, (as it is by the young British, and these include increasing numbers of young women)? For whatever else is put on the digital highway, it will undoubtedly include the contents of the old major storehouses of national identity – libraries, galleries and even television stations – which will be able to be reconfigured in unimaginable ways. Perhaps this might presage a new campaign around national literacy within Britain, focusing not on literacy in the old sense but on *literacy about the nation*. For the importance of the new screens is not merely that they have the potential to disseminate and democratise knowledge about the nation. They remind us all of the provisionality of what appears on them, and of our power to act on them in ways that may aid us. This electronic world may provide us with an opportunity to imagine British national identity not as something immovable as a monument nor something that needs to be tended as a lawn but as something as provisional and capable of transformation as a wave; a wave which we all might ride.

Bibliography

Anderson, Benedict (1983)
 Imagined Communities.
 Reflections on the Origin and
 Spread of Nationalism
 London, Verso

Ascherson, Neal (1988) *Games*
 with Shadows London, Radius

Barnett, Anthony (1982) *Iron*
 Britannia: Why Parliament
 Waged Its Falklands War
 London, Allison and Busby

Barnett, Correlli (1986)
 The Audit of War London,
 Macmillan

Calder, Angus (1981)
 Revolutionary Empires. The Rise of
 the English Speaking Empires
 from the Fifteenth Century to the
 1780's London, Jonathan Cape

Calder, Angus (1994)
 Revolving Culture: Notes from the
 Scottish Republic London, New
 York, IB Tauris

Calder, Angus (1969) *The People's*
 War 1939-45 London, Cape

Campbell, Beatrix 'This Grim
 Fairy Tale', *The Guardian*
 4 September 1992

Colley, Linda (1992) *Britons:*
 Forging the Nation 1707-1837
 Newhaven and London,
 Yale UP

Colls, Robert/Dodd, Philip
 (Eds) (1986) *Englishness: Politics*
 and Culture 1880-1920 London,
 Croom Helm

Cairns, Craig (1984)
 'George Orwell and the
 English Ideology'
 Cencrastus, Summer issue

Foster, R.F. (1993) *Paddy and*
 Mr Punch: Connections in
 Irish and English History
 London, Allen Lane

Fryer, Peter (1984) *Staying Power.*
 The History of Black People in
 Britain London and Sydney,
 Pluto

Gilroy, Paul (1987) *There Ain't No*
 Black in the Union Jack:
 The Cultural Politics of Race
 and Nation London Hutchinson

Gilroy, Paul (1993) *The Black*
 Atlantic: Modernity and Double
 Consciousness London,
 New York, Verso

Hall, Stuart (1991) 'Old and New Identities, Old and new Ethnicities' in *Culture Globalisation and the World System* ed Anthony D King Basingstoke, Macmillan

Holmes, Colin (1988) *John Bull's Island: Immigration and British Society 1871-1971* Basingstoke, Macmillan Education

Howkins, Alun *The Discovery of Rural England* in Colls and Dodd

Hobsbawm Eric/Ranger Terence (1983) *The Invention of Tradition* Cambridge, Cambridge UP

Nairn, Tom (1981) *The Break-Up of Britain* Second Expanded Edition London, Verso

Nairn, Tom (1988) *The Enchanted Glass: Britain and Its Monarchy* London, Radius

Newman, Gerald (1987) *The Rise of English Nationalism: A Cultural History 1740-1830* London, Weidenfield and Nicolson

Orwell, George (1941) *The Lion and the Unicorn: Socialism and the English Genius* London, Secker & Warburg Harmondsworth, Peguin

Perkin, Harold (1989) *The Rise of Professional Society: England Since 1880* London and New York, Routledge

Samuel, Raphael 'Sources of Marxist History' *New Left Review* No. 120

Samuel, Raphael (1989) (Ed) *Patriotism: The Making and Unmaking of British National Identity* London and New York, Routledge

Samuel, Raphael (1994) *Theatres of Memory* London, Verso

Smith, Alan G.R. (1984) *The Emergence of a Nation State: The Commonwealth of England 1529-1660* London and New York, Longman

Scannell, Paddy/Cardiff, David (1991) *A Social History of British Broadcasting: Serving the Nation vol 1 1922-39* Oxford, Basil Backwell

Smith, Anthony (1993), *Books to Bytes: Knowledge and Information in the Post-modern Era* London, BFI

Shawcross, William (1992) *Rupert Murdoch: Ringmaster of the Information Circus* London, Chatto and Windus

Starkey David 'Daze of Empire' *The Guardian* 11 January 1995

Thompson, E.P (1963) *The Making of the English Working Class* London, Gollancz

Wilson, Elizabeth (1985) *Adorned in Dreams* London, Virago

Wiener, Martin (1981) *English Culture and the Decline of the Industrial Spirit 1850-1980* Cambridge, Cambridge UP

Wright, Patrick (1985) *On Living in an Old Country: The National Past in Contemporary Britain* London, Verso

Williams, Gwyn A. (1985) *When Was Wales?* London, Black Raven

Young, Hugo (1989) *One of Us: A Biography of Margaret Thatcher* London, Macmillan

Acknowledgements

With thanks to:
Sophie Powell
Libby Fawbert
Duncan Petrie